Senior Adult Theatre

Prepared under the auspices of the ATA Senior Adult Theatre Program Committee, this Handbook should be useful to all those involved in some type of senior adult theatre program or planning to develop one.

It contains concrete suggestions for starting and developing all types of theatre experiences for senior adults.

SENIOR ADULT THEATRE

The American
Theatre Association Handbook

Edited by
Roger Cornish and C. Robert Kase

Contributors
Roger Cornish, C. Robert Kase, Paul Kozelka,
Horace W. Robinson, and Loren Winship

THE PENNSYLVANIA STATE UNIVERSITY PRESS
UNIVERSITY PARK AND LONDON

Library of Congress Cataloging in Publication Data

Main entry under title:

Senior adult theatre.
Includes Bibliography.
    1. Amateur theatricals.   2. Aged—Recreation.
I. Cornish, Roger.   II.   Kase, Charles Robert.
III.   American Theatre Association.
PN3156.S4   792'.0222   80–23485
ISBN 0–271–00276–X
ISBN 0–271–00275–1 (pbk.)

Contents

Contributors

Roger Cornish is Associate Professor of Theatre and Film at The Pennsylvania State University, where he is also an Associate of the Gerontology Institute. Editor and coauthor of *Short Plays for the Long Living,* he teaches dramatic writing and directs his department's graduate programs.

Paul Kozelka, Professor Emeritus and retired Chairman of the Department of Theatre, Columbia University Teachers College, has been President of the American Theatre Association. A Fellow of the Association, he was the first Chairman of its Committee on Senior Adult Theatre.

C. Robert Kase, a past President and Fellow of the American Theatre Association, whose Award of Merit he won in 1976, was Chairman of the Department of Theatre at the University of Delaware. Currently Chairman of ATA's Senior Adult Theatre Committee, Professor Kase is well known for his part in starting the American College Theatre Festival.

Horace W. Robinson, former Head of the Department of Theatre and Professor Emeritus of the University of Oregon, served as President of the American Theatre Association in 1954, received its

Award of Merit in 1977, and is an ATA Fellow. Twice a Fulbright Grant winner, he has been theatre architecture consultant on the construction of many university theatres.

The late *Loren Winship*, a Fellow of the American Theatre Association, won its Award of Merit in 1968. Long Chairman of the Theatre Department of the University of Texas, Professor Winship served as Managing Editor of the *Educational Theatre Journal* from 1949 to 1952.

All the contributors are members of the American Theatre Association Senior Adult Theatre Program Committee.

Foreword

The American Theatre Association, its leadership and members, recognize that they have much to share in a human development movement nurturing interaction between older Americans and their creative selves. ATA's *Senior Adult Theatre Handbook* testifies to this interest and illuminates ways by which older adults can enter the exciting world of the theatre arts. The *Handbook* will do much to stimulate theatre artists to work with older persons and encourage practitioners in the field of aging to support these innovative projects. But by no means is this a one-way relationship. Older Americans bring with them a range of talents and skills; they can contribute to theatre projects as artists, workers, students, teachers, creators, as well as audiences.

The growth in numbers of older citizens during the twentieth century represents an outstanding achievement. But it brings substantial changes in society as a whole and enormous challenges for leaders in all fields of endeavor, including the arts. As the average life expectancy of United States citizens has risen, the number of years outside the labor force has increased markedly for a majority of older Americans. Time away from work has gradually come to be viewed not as time to be "filled full" of busy work, but as time to be "fulfilled." It is seen as time for new learning experiences, for developing new interests and skills (or pursuing those left dormant), and for designing new strategies for re-engaging older persons in community life.

The rapid growth of the 65-and-over population, the decline in both the elderly mortality rate and the birthrate, indicate that our society is aging. This is reflected in the median age changes of the total population. In 1960, the median age was 29.5 years; by 1970, it had declined to 27.9 years; but, in the early 1980s, projections are that 30.3 years will be the median age. If one also considers that the age group 65 and over will expand by approximately thirty percent by the end of the century, then we are clearly in the midst of a demographic shift that must dictate a societal focus on the problems and potentials of an increasing population of older citizens.

The experience of the National Center on Arts and the Aging of the National Council on the Aging proves that older Americans are eager to take up new or renewed interest in the cultural and artistic life of our nation—as spectators or participants—whenever afforded meaningful opportunities to do so. We congratulate the American Theatre Association and all those who made this book possible. It is a welcomed addition to the growing body of literature promoting new dimensions to life in old age.

Jacqueline T. Sunderland
Director, National Center on Arts
and the Aging, National Council on
the Aging, Inc., Washington, D. C.

Preface

The American Theatre Association first addressed the subject of senior adult theatre in 1973, when Vera Mowry Roberts, then Association President, asked Paul Kozelka to chair the Association's first committee on theatre for retirees. First appointees to the committee were Dina Rees Shaw, Marjorie Dycke, Vera Roberts, James Butler, C. R. Kase, and Loren Winship. By 1977, Senior Adult Theatre had achieved the status of an Association Program, and its Committee has since counted among its members Horace Robinson, Kenneth Graham, Patricia Sawyer, Shirley Harbin, David France, Claire Michaels, Joseph Bellinghiere, Victoria Tate, and Father Gilbert V. Hartke. Serving ex officio for the past two years has been Jeanne Adams Wray, ATA Vice President for Programs.

In 1978, commissioned by the Kennedy Center's Alliance for Arts Education, members of the Committee and the national office of the Association conducted the Senior Adult Theatre Project, a wide-ranging survey of senior adult theatre activities around the country. The Association issued the survey report, *Older Americans on Stage,* in 1979.

The *Handbook* you are now reading is another offshoot of the Senior Adult Theatre Program's thrust to inform theatre people of what is possible and needful in theatre for seniors. Having succeeded Paul Kozelka as Committee Chairman, C. R. Kase made the publication of this first guide to senior adult theatre a primary goal of the Program. In addition to his fellow contributors, a number of people aided Kase mightily in forwarding the *Handbook*. Jack Morrison, ATA's Executive Director, gave early support to the idea of issuing the *Handbook* under ATA sponsorship, and Paul Antonie Distler shepherded the manuscript through the Association's Publications Committee. Well-known actor Salem Ludwig, artistic director of Dramature, encouraged the Penn State Press to adopt the project. The Press's John Pickering, a true humanist, had the insight to recognize the value in a book on senior adult theatre when the manuscript was still in very rough form.

Library shelves are not yet crowded with books on senior adult theatre as they are with, say, children's theatre books. This is quite natural; many of the basics of senior adult theatre are still to be learned, will only be learned when many more theatre people have dedicated significant amounts of time to practice in the field. In the meantime, this small volume and a few others mentioned in the bibliography may stand as the beginning of such a crowded shelf.

Roger Cornish

I

Introduction

C. Robert Kase and Roger Cornish

Today in the United States there are some thirty million citizens over 60 years of age. Their physical and economic welfare is the concern of numerous public and private agencies whose size and influence grow steadily. But only in recent years has there arisen concern for the humane quality of the lives of senior Americans, that quality which depends on access to the best our culture has produced in art and thought. Even now, the world of art—especially serious art—hardly touches the lives of most of our elderly. Reporting to the Senate Special Sub-committee on Aging in 1978, the National Endowment for the Arts confirmed this:

> Perhaps the most persistent barrier to developing quality arts programs for older Americans is that the public at large, and arts administrators and artists in particular, do not fully understand the relationship of the arts to individuals over 65 years of age.

Yet it is from the arts that our elderly citizens can derive fun, pleasure, and personal fulfillment, and in none of the arts is this more notable than in theatre.

This *Handbook* seeks to address two main groups: theatre artists who may become involved in leading theatre projects for older persons, and professional workers with the elderly so that they will be better prepared to recruit and cooperate with theatre artists by having some idea of what senior adult theatre (SAT) involves. Theatre artists may include those working with the CTAA Senior Adult Program Committee and other ATA divisional and regional SAT committees. The *Handbook* can also be helpful to any group of senior citizens interested in starting a theatre program.

But this is not a textbook. It is rather a guide to the different kinds of theater programs for the elderly and a compendium of the ways in which such programs can be developed. Perhaps it should be called a descriptive catalog of SAT activities, showing workers in retirement centers, nursing homes, and congregate meal and recreation centers ways in which their programs for the elderly might be enriched.

The implementation of an SAT program, however, cannot be effected without outside help by the average professional worker with the elderly. It requires the practical leadership of a theatre-trained person with experience in mounting shows, training inexperienced performers, or both. The role of the gerontology professional is to understand what theatre can do, to identify and recruit the theatre-wise leader, either on a paid or

Director Stuart Kandell starts a rehearsal of the College Avenue Players, a senior adult theatre group in Oakland, California. (Photo. by Deborah Maizels)

a volunteer basis, and to facilitate the work of that person by providing a fertile creative environment and the material support that the chosen theatre activities may require.

For both the theatre leader and the cooperating gerontology professional, this *Handbook* will review basic strategies for introducing senior adults to the theatre and will discuss the advantages and challenges involved in the various program approaches available.

The first chapters deal in the main with starting an SAT group and with the chief artistic lines that may be pursued profitably with seniors: standard production, readers' theatre, and creative drama or improvisation. Thereafter, the *Handbook* considers ancillary matters including senior adult audience programs, budgeting, and play selection.

4

It should be noted that the several contributors, each of whom is a theatre professional of different background, and each of whom has worked in senior adult theatre under different circumstances, will not always agree in approach or emphasis. But it is the nature of theatre art to accommodate many truths, and senior adult theatre will no doubt prove to be equally multifarious. There will always be more than one right way to do it; the key is to do it.

II

Getting Started

Paul Kozelka

Every senior adult drama group starts with a single live-wire, someone who knows how acting can give new energy and insight to the actor and pleasure and social benefits to the audience. This person is a catalyst, a leader whose enthusiasm makes people want to join in the fun. This self-starter or spark-plug may also be the director of plays after the group is organized, but the combination is not necessary. This leader may be a man or a woman, an outsider or a member of the group. Whichever the case, the first thing our live-wire must do is investigate and make some decisions: what kind of group will he work with, what kinds of theatre experience are possible, and what are the requirements for a successful theatre experience?

6

Entering the World of Senior Adults

As a leader, you may be called upon to work in a residential or a non-residential setting. Residential settings include retirement centers, mobile home or trailer camp communities, and residential care settings and nursing homes. The advantages here are that it is easy to make announcements and that you can depend on people for rehearsals and performances except when sudden illness occurs. In addition, these places often have a stage, a recreation fund to pay royalties and buy play-books, and lounges or rooms for reading, rehearsing, or performing.

The residential population is more or less captive and there are relatively few outside distractions, so theatre activity is welcomed as a healthy diversion and relief from routine. In nursing homes it is possible to involve wheelchair-bound actors who might never show up in non-residential settings. One Baltimore nursing home produced a successful fashion show satire in which models were played by both ambulatory and wheelchair actresses.

In all likelihood, the longest lived senior adult theatre group in the country is a residential group, the Youngtown Players, who have enlivened things in their Arizona retirement community since 1959 under the leadership of Dina Rees Shaw.

By non-residential groups, I mean senior centers, nutrition centers where senior adults gather for recreational activities after lunches served by local Meals on Wheels programs, church or temple groups, and AARP and other retirement organization chapters. These groups meet daily or regularly like clubs. Sometimes the members have many outside distractions and activities, but sometimes the senior center is their only source of recreation and social contact.

Administrators and recreation directors for resident and non-resident groups alike will welcome a qualified leader who wishes to start a theatre group, but the problem is to find actors with a modicum of ability and a good ratio of men to women actors. A leader should also remember that sometimes it takes many weeks of patience, exhortation, cajolery, flattery, legal bribery, and long periods of trial and error before a group takes off.

Whether it's an ad-hoc group organized on a temporary basis around one production or an on-going group with a regular program of varied theatre activities, our live-wire should remain flexible and adjust quickly to changing conditions. He can't expect the obedience and punctuality he found in educational or professional theatre.[1] Instead, he will find eager, appreciative, earnest amateurs who respond well to tactful criticism and who learn quickly to cooperate and submerge stubborn egos to the good of the group.

1. Although the authors recognize the leadership roles played by many women in SAT activities, the masculine pronoun is used for convenience.

8

Varieties of Theatre Experience

The easiest kind of theatre is the improvisation, which requires no memorization, usually has no audience, and is an excellent training technique for inexperienced actors. A few people may begin by discussing problems, which for older people may be loneliness, being a shut-in, financial problems, sex, depression, or irritability. Eventually, the leader encourages members to take certain roles or characters and act out the problems with words and actions.

Improvisation teaches actors how to listen, how to stay in character, how to develop conflicts, and how to resolve them. On occasion the leader can give the exercise a certain dramatic or artistic form by suggesting a logical beginning, middle and end; a specific conflict; and possible characterizations. Improvisations may be shared with audiences, but their main purpose is to "warm up" actors, to break through their armor of self-consciousness, and to start their imaginations flowing.

Another form of theatre that offers great aesthetic and intellectual satisfaction is play-reading. Start with one-act plays, and in two or three one-hour sessions, you can read a farce, a tragedy, a fantasy, and a melodrama. After readings, the members may discuss, for example, the various meanings they find in a play or in other works by the same author. Although the audience may request louder readings during this stimulating event, only the director should criticize individual performances.

The live-wire may decide that reader's theatre is the best form to start with, because his neighbors and friends may say they are interested in a theatre group but are positive they "can't memorize any more." (That isn't true; it just takes time.) In reader's theatre, performers sit on stools or stand behind music stands or lecterns and read from scripts, the leading characters being read by the same persons throughout and the minor characters assigned to one or two persons. A few rehearsals are necessary to develop interpretations and to establish some kind of contact between the actors, both physical and psychological.

Next comes script-in-hand production, in which actors develop characters and perform the action and business required by the play. Although they carry scripts, if the actors turn the pages unobtrusively and have rehearsed enough to create believable action, they can make the audience forget the scripts. As in reader's theatre, some actors may read several small roles, or sections of the play may be cut, with a narrator providing the bridges. As in other kinds of informal theatre, a master of ceremonies can welcome the audience, encourage it to use its imagination, and describe the settings they should envision.

Very different is the vaudeville or variety show, which requires a minimum of rehearsal time and a maximum of organizing ability on the part of the director or play committee. The show may consist of popular songs with new lyrics that refer to local personalities or events, plus original sketches or parodies of current TV programs. Some groups have a great time with a minimum of rehearsal by

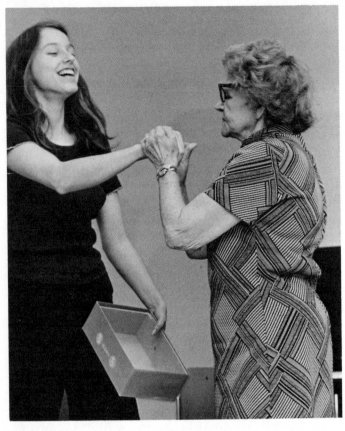

Pamela Perkins of the Brookdale Drama Project, directed by Milton Polsky and sponsored by New York's Hunter College, gains the confidence of an aspiring senior actress.

dramatizing jokes or acting out cartoons from magazines and newspapers. "Most seniors here like something they can do fast and get a laugh," said one California correspondent.

What people think of when you say theatre, of course, is the memorized play, with or without a genuine stage, scenery, and lighting. Most people like to act as they like to sing, but polished acting talent is scarce. Nevertheless, a creative director can make a beginning actor look good if the actor will spend the necessary effort at rehearsals and at home. And there is no greater thrill for a director or audience than seeing an older adult do some acting for the first time in his life and do it successfully.

The Elements of Good Theatre

Now that the spark plug has drawn some conclusions about the type of group and the type of theatre experience he wants to lead, he must do a little exploring for a director, a meeting place, highly motivated actors, potential audiences, and behind-the-scenes workers.

The leader may also be the director, but that isn't necessary. But whatever the case, the presence of a strong director is all-important. According to the nationwide study of senior adult theatre groups carried out by the American Theatre Association's Senior Adult Theatre Program, the most successful senior groups have been those blessed with clearly identified, theatre-wise directors.[2]

2. *Older Americans on Stage*, report to the Alliance for Arts Education of the Kennedy Center, Washington, D. C.

Some senior groups have been led by younger people such as Susan Rowland of Louisville's Senior Players. Other senior groups have been directed by contemporaries like Dina Rees Shaw, who guided the very successful Youngtown Players of Youngtown, Arizona for twenty years after her retirement from theatre teaching.

The director who works with seniors needs tact, patience, a strong will, and a clear knowledge of how the final result will sound and look, as well as a command of the techniques needed to produce those results. As the director of a group in a California retirement center says, "A director is needed so the skit, no matter how short, can be planned with some kind of action, with props if they are to be used, and so that the skit can be rehearsed according to plan, including entering and exiting, turning to others, speaking to the audience from various stage positions, because imparting 'stage secrets' makes for a better production and gives those on the stage more confidence."

The director should know enough about voice production to be able to help new actors project and give their lines a lifelike reality in an artificial situation. He should have different remedies, physical and psychological, for stagefright. He needs to know various ways to memorize and, above all, he needs to know when to interrupt a rehearsal to make corrections and when to let it continue so the actors may learn the flow of the play—and because the mistake will often disappear by itself. He should be flexible enough to teach by direct imitation, to serve as a model if necessary.

The director may be experienced in educational or professional theatre, may be a theatre student or a faculty member of a local high school or college. Whether the director should be paid or not is an open question. The best ones, to my knowledge, volunteer their services as their contribution to a cooperative effort.

Performance Space for the Senior Adult Theatre Group

Concurrently with recruitment, the director must secure an appropriate space to meet, rehearse, and perform. The average person probably thinks that a theatre program requires a fully equipped stage, but not only is such a plant unnecessary for many senior adult theatre projects, it might even create more problems than it would solve. For instance, many older people would have difficulty managing the vocal projection required by a large standard theatre.

I have found that an ordinary room is often the best locale for senior adult work. For example, I have successfully used the community room of a large cooperative apartment house for meetings and actual performances. About eighteen feet wide and thirty feet long, the room is converted into a theatre by the addition of two portable

The Third Age Theatre, based at the Ambler (Pennsylvania) Arts Center, goes on tour to a local senior activities center.

masking screens at one end of the rectangle. Because there is no raised stage in this room, actors must often stand to be seen during important speeches, but because the room is small, the senior audience hears with no difficulty, and that is of paramount importance.

Since the room is simply a flexible box, we occasionally locate our playing space along a side wall and seat the audience around it in two gentle curves. In either situation, we achieve the intimacy that is so important to senior audiences and players.

Dina Reese Shaw, who led the Youngtown Players for so many years, states that the greatest single need at this time is a theatre designed especially for senior audiences and performers. She recommends an acting area about fifteen feet square and a seating area of three deep bleachers on three sides of the acting area. The back wall may be left unadorned or trimmed with window frames or pictures. Such an arrangement would do much to solve the two chief problems of senior audiences, impaired vision and hearing.

Finally we come to the audience, which will turn the stage space into "living theatre." A retirement home, nutrition center, or nursing home provides a dependable, stable audience, but the possibilities of touring a show to other institutions are endless. Churches will welcome a seasonal nave drama from groups that perfrom plays with a religious tone. At clubs, singing groups and bands are always a welcome relief from old movies, but real live actors doing a good job with a good show are a stunning novelty. All it takes is someone to make the arrangements for travel.

The Initial Stimulus

Often the spark-plug who started this chapter is the one who starts the whole theatre group: a teacher or actor who has had training and experience spreads his enthusiasm through a group or neighborhood, arranges for some publicity, and at the first meeting promotes group decisions about goals, procedures, and schedules.

One very effective way to get senior adults started in dramatic activities is to recruit a few of the more adventuresome retirees to play older characters in community or university theatre productions. Once a few members of your senior community have gotten their feet wet, their excitement may prompt many others to take a chance.

Sometimes the stimulus may come from a visiting company of older actors. As they watch a visiting company of their contemporaries performing and receiving applause, some of the audience are likely to think, "We can do as well as they can, maybe better." Visiting performances can also be used to swell the size of an embryonic group. In Florida, the Canterbury Players started with only two actors and a director. The trio mounted a reader's theatre performance of Robert Anderson's *I'm Herbert,* performed it before an invited audience of older persons, and then took it on the road to senior centers. Within five months, the Canterbury Players had grown to a membership of forty-five.[3]

Another group that now produces three plays a year began as an informal play-reading group. They read Susan Glaspell's *Trifles,* a suspense

3. New York City's Dramature, a group started by professional actors, employs a variation of this approach. Dramature made its debut by taking a production of Arthur Miller's *The Price* to New York's Jewish Home and Hospital for the Aged. Having excited its audience with the performance and post-performance discussion, Dramature then provided a theatre director, Vivian King, to lead the newly interested residents into their own original theatrical production. Editor's Note (RC).

story of Minnie Wright, whom we never see because she is in jail on suspicion of murdering her
husband. Two neighbors, who describe Minnie as
a quiet, loveable soul, destroy incriminating evi-
dence against her, a dead canary with a twisted
neck. After the play-reading, the audience discussion proved so spirited that one member wrote his
own sequel, *The Trial of Minnie Wright*. What better motivation to establish a producing group?

Get Started, Please!

But enough of this talk. It's time for action. Get
started! No matter how informal the activity may
be and no matter what form of theatre you culti-
vate, give it a decent chance. If it catches on and
everyone survives the low periods just before
dress rehearsal and remembers the exaltation that
comes from satisfying an audience and taking curtain calls, then there is plenty of time to draw up a
constitution, prepare a directory of members,
elect a treasurer and apply for an IRS exemption,
appoint a play-reading committee, and select a
name.

There are pleasures, opportunities, and adventures ahead, so get started—please.

III

Senior Adults in Play Production

Horace Robinson

This chapter is designed to assist knowledgeable theatre practitioners who wish to develop play production programs involving senior adult participants. Such programs may enlist seniors in interaction with the younger members of broad-based community groups, such as college or high school theatres, or in exclusively senior adult theatre projects. Most of the observations to follow will apply in either case.

With senior adults, all the processes of theatre—play selection, rehearsal, and performance—should be thought of as meaningful and exciting social experience that makes every theatre day rewarding, not just the day the performer faces the audience. Therefore, it is probably better for the senior adult theatre groups not to set too early deadlines or performance dates. A quality performance experience is desirable, but seniors should not be so pressured with impending performances that they cannot savor fully every moment of preparation for the production experience. Senior adult theatre is at its best when it is truly process-oriented, so preparation should last as long as it is stimulating.

Even after the show is over, the process should continue to reward senior participants. Performers and audiences should get together for post-performance appreciations of production decisions, performances, and the play's relevance to the life of the audience. A good theatre experience continues to live by prompting thought and discussion by everyone involved.

Full Participation

Senior adult theatre is best thought of as participant-oriented. Too much of the senior life experience encourages passivity, and, thereby, decay. But theatre for senior adults is a pull to active, energetic effort. Naturally, audiences must be considered, but even the benefits senior audiences will derive from a performance will be a factor of the amount of active senior participation they see on stage and backstage—theatre *by* seniors can encourage renewed sense of life potential *in* seniors. Consequently, attention should be given to all the possibilities for active senior participation.

Even the process of play selection can pleasurably involve a sizeable group of senior adults. And the choice of a play with only seven characters, say, can open opportunities for fifteen or twenty people in backstage and front-of-house activities.

As far as acting is concerned, participation can be broadened by multiple casting. Several roles may be played by more than one person. It is not advisable, however, to use the term *understudy*; the term *alternate* is better. Alternates who are assured the opportunity to play in even one performance can maintain a strong interest in developing roles. If sufficient actors are available, entire separate casts may be rehearsed for alternating performances, or different cast combinations may be selected for each performance. Mild but energizing competition can be so developed, but actors playing the same role should be encouraged to develop their own interpretations rather than carbon-copy performances. By this means, the audience may even be tempted to attend several performances to compare the work of different casts.

In another approach, casts and audiences alike may enjoy a performance in which single roles are played at different moments by different actors. Although none of the participants in such multiple casting schemes are called understudies, it is obvious that emergency standbys are thereby provided. Another advantage of multiple casting is that two or more groups of actors can be supported with a single setting, one lighting set-up, one set of properties, one publicity campaign, and—if he or she has the stamina—one director. In Topeka, Kansas, the Barn Theatre developed a special production, *The Theatre Looks at Aging,* and

Ideas for an original play are developed by Oakland's College Avenue Players, inspired by their director's visual aids. (Photo by Deborah Maizels)

then formed six companies of over-fifty-year-old actors who were able to perform the show on request for an unlimited number of clubs or community organizations.[1]

Finally, it should also be obvious that any or all of the non-acting chores—with the possible exception of directing—lend themselves to shared responsibility. Even if there is only enough work for one person in a crew position such as property head or ticket taker, these jobs may be shared by

1. There is another advantage to the use of alternates. My experience has shown the desirability of having alternates for all parts, although one person can serve as alternate for several parts. Senior adults are more subject to illness than younger persons, and the alternate system helps avoid disruption of either rehearsals or performances due to absences. Editor's Note (CRK)

alternation to provide more opportunities for participation of a less demanding nature.

Having encouraged the provision of many participating opportunities for seniors, this writer concludes that senior adult projects are best organized on a modest basis. Large senior groups invariably encounter problems in communication, prolonged vacations, and competing activities. While it is conceivable that a large pageant or spectacle involving a hundred or more senior adults might be successfully organized for religious, charitable, or political purposes, long-range plans should be based on more modest groups of ten to twenty people.

The small group makes collective endeavour much simpler. Ten or twelve members can be transported in only two cars. A meeting place can be made of a private living room. And the likelihood of finding working hours convenient for all is much greater in a modest group. Perhaps more important, the comradeship so essential for senior work will be much easier to achieve within a group whose participants are all on a first-name basis.

Modes of Involvement

Whatever the group's size, its members should have the opportunity to participate in every aspect

An original play script is studied by two participants in Rae Edelson's playwrighting workshop of the Brookdale Drama Project. (Photo by Terry Buchalter, courtesy of Milton Polsky)

of theatre activity. And a surprising number of those activities may have particular validity for members of a senior troupe.

Playwriting

The theatre experience may be even more exciting if the play is written by a member of the group rather than picked from play catalogs. The production of original scripts is an important aspect of the work of many of the senior companies now operating. Some groups, such as San Francisco's Tale Spinners, have written their own scripts about aging in order to explode some myths about growing old. Other groups, such as Chicago's Free Street Too and New York's Dramature, have made plays from the rich vein of oral history that runs through the memories of the elderly. Local history, personal adventures, nostalgia can be developed into short dramatic episodes to make an interesting dramatic program. In a well-coordinated ensemble, the actors can help polish up shaky dialogue. Playwriting is essentially storytelling, and seniors are good storytellers because they wish to share their rich experience with others.

Technical Theatre and Design

Many of the elderly possess specific skills that can be turned to good account in the scene shop and backstage. Though lighting design is a highly technical field, the weekend electrician can perform many services such as repairing cable, cleaning lenses, or rewriting cue sheets. Costuming need not even require the presence of the older worker in the shop. Many an elderly needleworker can do better beading or lace application in her own home than could be procured for pay from a commercial seamstress.

As for property construction and scene decoration, many senior adults who have no theatre experience are blessed with skills the theatre can use. Retired sheet metal workers, machinists, and carpenters will be pleased to contribute their talents to a show. Instead of being content with what comes out of the local junk shop or the director's attic, why not let the retired plumber build the practical sink unit you need or invite a retired local artist to craft original set ornaments? In Fort Wayne, Indiana, the Civic Theatre recruited seniors to do regular shop stints for all its productions.

Promotion and Publicity

Less theatrical but just as valuable to any show are promotion, publicity, and sales. Senior adults who have spent a lifetime in business can be invaluable in dealing with newspapers, developing displays, conducting telephone campaigns, marking and racking tickets, or laying out programs.[2] And any theatre can make good use of a methodical historian. The elderly usually have a strong sense of heritage, and they can sense that the trivia of today may be valuable historical artifacts in the future.

Assistant Director

In many cases, the actual director of a senior adult theatre production will not be a group member

2. A printed or typed program can make the performance more enjoyable for members of the audience, and it is often appreciated by members of the cast and staff who may want to send copies to sons, daughters, grandchildren, and friends. Programs can be reproduced from typewritten copy by photocopying machines, which are usually available. Editor's Note (CRK)

26

but an outsider. In such cases, an assistant director enlisted from within the group can maintain liaison with group members and carry on rehearsals when the director is not there. This procedure also provides training for a group member who may eventually take over the reins of regular directing, either because a guest director is not available or because the assistant has naturally matured to the point where direction is the appropriate next step.

Space for Senior Adult Theatre

Working space is often a problem for senior performance groups. A Fairfax County, Virginia, program reported to the Senior Adult Theatre Project that it had been forced out of existence because it had been unable to obtain a suitable space convenient to its members. Other groups report problems with host organizations such as senior activity centers which are unable to provide working space that is free of distractions or interference.

But such problems tend to diminish with the realization that senior groups do not necessarily require either a particular kind of theatre space or even a formal theatre space of any kind. Where box office income is not a factor, rewarding performances can be staged in living rooms, church basements, schoolrooms, or retirement home lounges. Some senior groups have taken variety shows into hospital wards. The place of senior adult theatre is of little consequence as long as the participants adjust their performances to the physical surroundings and establish satisfactory relationships with their audiences.

The most important consideration is the ability of the audience to see and hear. For this reason, the proscenium stage or a similarly laid out informal space is generally thought best for seniors. The actors should be able to direct voice and gesture toward the entire audience at all times.[3]

Choosing Material for Senior Adult Performance

In choosing material, there are two major considerations: first, what are the benefits to be derived from rehearsal and related activity; and, second, what are the benefits to be derived from performance and related activity? The former question is to be answered in terms of the participants alone,

3. In case there is no elevated stage area, platforms can be rented or made. Portable and collapsible, they can be stored between uses. Platforms should be at least 12 inches high, though 24 inches is better. There should be a step or steps to avoid the possibility of accidents. Editor's Note (CRK)

Pinocchio, with five senior adults in a cast of fifteen, is presented in an Austin elementary school by the Theatre For Youth Series of The University of Texas Drama Department.

but the latter must be answered with some regard to the needs of the audience.

The most common mistake in senior programming is to underestimate time requirements, both for preparation and for performance. A preparation period envisioned as two weeks stretches to four or six, and a performance planned for an hour swells to an hour-and-a-half. *Think small*, at least until you have carefully explored the physical, mental, and social resources of your group. Even if your senior players are very hale and capable of extended hard work, remember that your audiences, should you perform for retirement or nursing home residents, may not have the vitality required for sustained concentration that is made more difficult by an unaccustomed need to sit still for an hour or more.

Most groups will select their material from published plays found in royalty catalogs. Chapter VI offers guidelines for identifying such material and obtaining performance rights.

But seniors should not feel obligated to use the entire script of a play selected. Judicious cutting may shorten a play by eliminating sub-plots or less important characters or even make a complete dramatic unit of one act of a three-act play. An otherwise difficult play may be made suitable by cutting, changing the setting, or modifying the age, sex, or physical characteristics of characters in the play. If the play is not in the public domain and the production is to be offered to the public, permission for major alterations should be sought from the publisher.

Indeed, the best choice for senior groups may well be the one-act play, which seniors may perform as brief offerings or in combinations of two or three short plays to make a longer show. In either case, the choice of the one-acter reduces rehearsal time and places less stress on the performance powers of inexperienced seniors while at the same time providing cast and audience a complete dramatic experience. Many successful senior groups report relying heavily on one-acters, especially groups that tour their productions to senior residences and activity centers, because the one-acter is the ideal length for the after-lunch program that touring groups often provide.

An even less taxing presentation may be constructed from scenes taken from well-known plays. Several scenes varying in length from three to fifteen minutes can provide performance opportunities for several small groups of actors without overburdening any individual. The director can tailor such scenes to the talents of individual performers, prepare with minimum rehearsal time, and produce with no more material support than a few costume and prop pieces. At the same time, such cameo selections allow each performer to shine for his or her moments on stage without having to negotiate a full rehearsal process.

Also useful as performance material are sketches—short comic bits which are often variations on a well-known theme and involve little or no character or plot development. They are seen frequently on such television shows as "Saturday Night Live." The format is familiar, the characterizations are broad, and little is demanded of the performer in terms of finesse or subtlety. A sketch, like a joke, demands something of the teller but probably requires less special training than any of the other forms mentioned. Books of sketches are available from most play publishers. The sketch also is possibly the simplest material for beginners to write. Local situations in government or society, well-known individuals, or social conventions such as those of marriage or parenthood are good subjects for the sketch. Sketches may be written by individuals or built out of the contributions of a creative group.

Serious theatre professionals will tend to think in terms of dramatic performance in choosing material. But they should be aware that many senior groups have found success in variety performance, especially in the formative stages of their organizations. Whereas senior groups are often totally lacking in dramatic experience, they usually number among their members people with experience in musical performance, not to mention people who can do card tricks, clown, or perform ethnic dances. And the variety format allows senior adults to build upon vaudeville and church social models of their earlier years. In building a show around the popular songs of their youth, elderly performers make a virtue of their age, enjoy nostalgia themselves, and offer a younger audience a glimpse of an earlier time. A group at the Jewish Home and Hospital for the Aged in New York City, helped by a director from Dramature, developed a musical show by combining old favorite songs with Lower East Side memories.

Some groups mix dramatic and variety formats. In Spokane, Washington, Project Joy has organized its members into subgroups, some of which are primarily dramatic, some primarily variety. And in Fort Washington, Pennsylvania, the Third Age Theatre inserts musical interludes between the one-act plays that form the core of its productions.

Readers Theatre

The common factor of all forms of readers theatre is the absence of memorization, a distinct advantage for senior adults because they often experience anxiety at the thought of memorization (though they can usually do it). Several readers theatre variants serve senior adults well. At one end of the spectrum, plays may be fully produced in every way except that the performers carry scripts from which they may regularly read or merely refresh their memories. Such productions, generally referred to as script-in-hand, may feature complete scenery, properties, and costumes, or may rely on a simple furniture arrangement to suggest the environment. After several rehearsals for such a performance, players will find themselves increasingly free of the scripts, using them primarily for security and reference. In fact, at moments of complicated business or stage action, the actors may put their scripts completely aside, taking care only to save their places with bookmarks.

Other styles of readers theatre eschew obvious theatrical trappings in favor of an experience shared between actor and audience. Actors interpret lines to suggest nuances of character, mood, and situation, but perform little or no stage movement. When such a style is chosen, the director should give careful thought to whether his performers should stand at reading stands throughout or retire to chairs during periods when their characters are out of action.

In such minimal performances, the director can enhance the presentation by casting one of his performers as a narrator or interlocutor who introduces the play, describes the setting, identifies characters, narrates pertinent business, and otherwise moves the performance forward.

The director of readers theatre for seniors should keep several points in mind. First, many senior groups do unrehearsed play readings as a means of experiencing dramatic literature in a vivid and social way. However, such cold readings have little audience appeal, and this approach should be kept in camera; untrained seniors should not be asked to capture an audience where even professionals would fail.

Second, because hearing loss is the single most frequently reported health problem among senior adults, the director must make every effort to develop constant good projection and to ensure that the performance environment is free from competing noise. Don't expect to achieve a good readers theatre experience in a day room in which other activities are going on or which serves as a main traffic artery for center business.

Third, keep performances short or provide frequent intermissions. Readers theatre, less visually dynamic than standard fare, can quickly exhaust the concentration capacities of elderly performers and audiences alike.

Along the same line, take care that scripts be not too bulky lest the audience become alarmed at the "two hundred pages yet to go." At the same time, try to arrange for large-type versions of the script so that your readers do not muffle their voices and obscure their expressions because they must bury their noses in the script in order to see it.

Not only is readers theatre an excellent compromise form for senior players, it can sometimes

Austin's "Act Your Age" program brings together senior and junior performers in *Star Spangled Minstrel*, directed by Joyce Chambers Selber.

serve as an intermediate step by which inexperienced seniors can be moved to standard dramatic performance. Arizona's Youngtown Players and the Hawthorne Players of Leesburg, Florida, both began as readers theatre groups and moved up to standard production as their members gained confidence.

Working Seniors Into Non-Senior Theatre

Theatre production offers recreation, therapy, and socialization to all participants, young and old. So valuable an activity can it be that it would be foolish to suggest that senior thespians are well served by senior companies only. An even better means of introducing senior adults to a valuable theatre experience may be to reach out and involve them significantly in the everyday theatrical life of the community. In high school productions, children's theatres, university theatres, and community theatres, seniors may lend maturity, authenticity, and a large measure of experience to roles in standard productions. Their potential for contributing to other areas of theatre production has already been discussed. Unfortunately, seniors are not likely to offer themselves uninvited. It is up to the theatre organizations to mount an outreach effort that moves into the senior center, the meal program, and the retirement community.

The greatest deterrent to the recruitment of seniors for community theatrical production appears to be the long list of misconceptions about seniors to which so many younger people subscribe. When you are presenting the case for seniors to your theatre group, make sure they don't assume that:

> —all seniors suffer memory loss and have a short attention span. Paul Boxell, director of Catonsville, Maryland's Autumn Players, reports that only three of twenty-five senior performers had serious memorization problems, and only one of those had finally to give it up. On the contrary, some of the best memorizers of the Autumn Players were among the eldest participants.
>
> —have failing eyesight, suffer bad health, and

tire easily. Again, the Autumn Players, one of the busiest and best reported senior touring groups, reports never having to miss a performance because of fatigue, illness, or any other reason.

—are reclusive, talk too much, are indigent, or have so many hobbies and other activities that they could not maintain a strong commitment.

Some of the elderly may have some of these problems, as may younger persons, but individuals of all ages deserve the opportunity to do creative work.

IV

Improvisational Drama with Senior Adults

Roger Cornish

If you are a trained theatre person planning to work with senior adults, the chances are good that you'll start with an already extant group which you've been invited to serve—at a senior club such as an AARP chapter or at a congregate center for seniors such as a retirement home or a meal center operated by the local Meals on Wheels office. What follows is one approach—the improvisational approach—which you might take in such circumstances.

Be sure of one thing at the start: there is a definite need for your services to such groups. You'll meet in them a wide range of senior adults who could benefit from dramatic activities. In an AARP chapter, for example, you'll encounter recently retired people who are in most ways young and vital and need only a new focus of energy to maintain a high measure of vitality. You may provide that through drama. You will also encounter in congregate centers people in their eighties and nineties for whom dramatic activities may become a crucial life-line to continued communication and socialization.

Obviously, both kinds of seniors need leadership if they are to enjoy the benefits of dramatic activity. Just as obviously, that leadership will usually have to come from outside the senior group. The seniors themselves are likely to be short of theatrical experience. Nor is it likely that congregate center staff members will be qualified to lead dramatic activities, because there is as yet no tradition of employing theatre-trained persons in even the larger centers. Those staff members who do specialize in arts activities are generally trained in the visual arts.

It's to be hoped that eventually the efforts of the theatre and gerontological communities will create a regular place for drama specialists in congregate centers. In the meantime, however, theatre professionals or students must be willing to fill the gap on a volunteer or paid consultant basis. The chances are good that you can fill such a role if you are prepared not to patronize senior adults but to work with them toward a standard of excellence as you would with any other adult group. Seniors, too often patronized in the marketplace and the home, don't need such condescension in the drama workshop.

The Improvisation Alternative

If you agree to lead a senior adult drama group, it will be for you to choose between the approaches of traditional production from scripts and improvisational drama.[1] The seniors themselves will probably assume that theatre means doing *Hello, Dolly* or *The Odd Couple*. If they have had experience, it will almost certainly have been in traditional production. But there are several reasons why you might consider basing your activities in improvisational drama.

First, improvisational drama addresses the positive goals of theatre for senior adults. Milton Polsky, Director of the Brookdale Drama Project, maintains that improvisation generally improves senior socialization and communication skills.[2] Improvising seniors are likely to improve habits of listening, responding aggressively to stimuli, and using the whole self for expression. One late-sixties woman in a workshop I directed had slipped over the years into a pattern of silent deference to her pleasant but dominating husband. In early workshop sessions she limited her contributions to monosyllables and regularly frustrated coaches by immediately surrendering to the wishes of her partner in any conflict improvisation. But, as the leaders persisted in drawing her out, her expressiveness, confidence, and will power grew until she became an effective, though not a leading, performer. Two years later, still working in occasional workshop sessions, she had retained the gains of the workshop and was a

1. To avoid the connotations of children's theatre often associated with the term *creative drama*, *improvisational drama* will be used throughout.

2. *The Brookdale Drama Project* (New York: unpublished Hunter College Report, Spring 1976.)

more outgoing, expressive person both on and off stage than she had been before she started.

Various observers also suggest that improvisational work is valuable as a means of using one's own experience to confront problems of senior adulthood. By improvising around such topics as death, money, the loss of loved ones, and isolation, seniors may increase their real coping skills. Naturally, seniors often choose escapist topics for improvisation—sex and violence are as popular over sixty as under. But when the topic is especially relevant to key life issues, improvisers grow through solving problems by their own decisions, not, as traditional actors do, by reference to the playwright. In a recent doctoral thesis, Barbara Davis reports that tests of a group of senior adults who participated in an improvisational drama workshop showed decreased levels of general anxiety and self-directed hostility.[3]

Second, several bothersome troubles sometimes associated with traditional theatre production by senior adults may be avoided through the improvisational approach. For example, there is a general shortage of good dramatic scripts especially suitable for performance by seniors. Further on, this *Handbook* offers a list of plays that may ameliorate the problem, but it's safe to say that it will be some time before seniors can select from a truly rich repertory of especially suitable plays. Improvisation eliminates the problem.

3. *Assessing the Impact of Creative Drama Training on Older Adults.* Unpublished Ph.D. dissertation, The Pennsylvania State University, 1980.

A more lasting problem associated with senior adult theatre is memorization, reported by Paula Gray to be one of the biggest problems in the New York City senior drama programs she examined.[4] While many maintain that the problem is not memorization itself but the fear of memorization—both among the elderly and among those who work with them—the problem exists and will persist until someone supplies an effective technique for dealing with it. In the meantime, improvisation neatly sidesteps the difficulty.

Another nettlesome problem in traditional production and readers theatre is failing eyesight. In residential settings where participants tend to be in the older strata of senior adults this handicap may be especially bothersome. Large-type scripts are hard to come by and expensive to produce. The improviser needn't worry.[5]

Finally, a myriad of tiny problems involved with traditional production—props, costumes, scenery, casting to type in realistic plays that call for various age ranges—are eliminated by the improvisational approach. Each performance is built from the capacities, characteristics, and resources of the group that creates it.

Traditional approaches are in no danger of being eliminated as senior adult theatre tools. However, the improvisational approach is taking its

4. *Dramatics for the Elderly: A guide for Directors of Dramatic Groups in Senior Centers and Residential Care Settings.* (New York: Columbia University Teachers College Press, 1974.)
5. Fairness requires acknowledgement that failing hearing is a bigger problem to improvisers than to actors in standard productions.

42

place as an important force, and there have been
some outstanding success stories in improvisational theatre for senior adults. In 1975, Patrick
Henry's Free Street Theatre in Chicago launched
Free Street Too, a group of performers who have
taken their group-improvised show, *To Life*, to
some twenty states. In 1978, Louisville's Actors
Theatre launched the Senior Players. An immediate hit, these 65 to 80-year-old improvisers were
soon booking three performances per week at
schools, hospitals, and clubs. Both groups draw
upon life experiences to reach audiences of all
ages. This writer's own book, *Short Plays for the
Long Living*, is the result of an improvisational theatre workshop sponsored by the Penn State Exten-
sion Service for 65 to 85-year-olds at Altoona,
Pennsylvania, congregate meal centers.[6]

In all, the American Theatre Association's Senior Adult Theatre Project Report estimates that
fifty per cent of all senior groups use improvisational techniques, if not as a performance base, at
least as a training tool. Particularly noted is the
fact that groups with professional leadership tend
even more toward the use of improvisational techniques than groups without qualified leaders. Several individuals who have earned national reputa-
tions for their work with senior adults rely heavily
on improvisation. The Brookdale Project's Milton
Polsky, Shirley Harbin of the Detroit Metropolitan
Theatre Council, and Isobel Berger of Maryland's

6. Free Street Theatre, 59 West Hubbard St., Chicago, Ill.,
60610; Actors Theatre, 316 W. Main St., Louisville, Ky.,
40202; John Orlock and Roger Cornish, *Short Plays for the
Long Living*, ed. Roger Cornish (Boston: Baker's Plays, 1976.)

College of Notre Dame all emphasize improvisational techniques.

Starting an Improvisational Workshop

Your first task will be recruiting a good group. Don't expect the center staff or club leaders to do it for you; they can post a sign-up sheet that residents may ignore, but they can't describe what you'll be doing or convey the sense of excitement that will attract enthusiastic members.

Therefore, once you've agreed to run an improvisational drama workshop, you should schedule a demonstration session in which you will preview your activities before a large gathering of seniors. Such a session should do two things: make the audience understand what improvisational drama is, and get *everyone* present to participate so they learn the activity is something they can do and enjoy.

If possible, enlist a partner of the oposite sex to give the demonstration with you. Senior men, whom it will be toughest to enlist, should see a masculine figure involved lest they be put off by prejudices about theatre and sex roles. And all your audience will benefit from seeing improvisational drama in the attractive light of the heterosexual group activity it is.

Senior adults are led in a warm-up exercise by Penn State's Joel Gori in the workshop room of the Altoona Library.

You may well start your session by improvising with your partner on situations volunteered by the audience. This will clarify the basic nature of improvisation better than any abstract explanation, and a few laughs will establish the happy mood you want.

Next, lead the audience through a series of exercises that represent the basic kinds of activities they'd pursue in an on-going workshop: physical warm-ups; ice-breakers and trust exercises; relaxation and concentration exercises; sensory awareness work; the full gamut of activities you will include in your regular sessions. Your primary goal should be to make every person in the room participate in at least some of the exercises. Obviously, time and temperament will prevent more than a few people telling a story or trying a rough improvisation; on the other hand, all fifty can join in the physical warm-up, do a relaxation exercise,

Members of the One Niter Senior Theatre Ensemble, directed by Bonnie L. Vorenberg, rehearse a dance in Eugene, Oregon. (Photo by Keith Allen)

or investigate a sensory stimulus such as the touch of the next person's hand.

Compared to genuine workshop efforts, such a session is necessarily superficial, but it may produce the excitement and sense of possibility that allow good recruitment. I always take care to point out that the audience is not being trained, merely introduced to improvisational drama.

Once you have enlisted a dozen or so workshop members, you'll need to work out a schedule. Naturally the membership will have a lot to say about when and how often the group should meet. Louisville's Senior Players meet for three four-hour sessions per week without feeling overtaxed, so you needn't worry that your seniors aren't up to more than the lightest schedule. And an eager group is likely to want to meet more than once a week. But it is important to see that the workshop does not interfere with other favorite activities, like scheduled bowling or bridge. Naturally you should not be surprised if members prefer to meet during the daylight hours.

As for location, almost any room of decent size will serve, but I prefer a room with no stage because sometimes seniors find it hard to disassociate improvisational drama from traditional theatre, and a stage will only encourage them to play for an imaginary audience instead of striving for honest interaction with other improvisers.

More important than the size and shape of the room is its privacy. Attaining concentration will be a major task of initial sessions and, in the absence of privacy, there will always be a few uncommitted seniors who will think it a good idea to pop in, kibbitz noisily, and distract group members from the work.

Areas of Special Attention for Seniors

If you've already done creative drama work, you probably have a game file full of exercises suitable for developing your senior group's skills. If not, Way, Spolin, and others provide many good exercises to use until your group develops its own.[7] Whatever specific exercises you choose, however, you should take care to include in every session five categories of work that promise special benefits for seniors: physical fitness warm-ups; relaxation; concentration; sensory awareness; and memory work.

Habitual physical exercise is one of the most important benefits of improvisational drama for seniors. But younger leaders may hesitate to supervise such exercises because they fear overtaxing or even injuring seniors, whom they imagine to be— usually without good cause—extremely frail. A good solution to this problem is recruiting a group member as exercise leader. In a group which I coordinated, a seventy-year-old had already established herself as a fitness guru at her senior center. Enlisting her aid assured that fitness work would be well adapted to seniors and also had the healthy effect of putting some leadership into the hands of the group.

Tension, as Way points out, is sometimes a byproduct of age and the preoccupations that may accompany it. Participation in such unfamiliar and challenging activities as drama may increase such tensions. Therefore, seniors should develop habits of releasing tensions through conscious relaxation techniques. Many of the best relaxation exercises—the sort you've done in acting classes—involve lying on the floor, but this may prove embarrassing or even impossible for some seniors. If

7. Brian Way, *Development Through Drama* (New York: Humanities Press, 1967), and Viola Spolin, *Improvisation for the Theatre* (Evanston: Northwestern University Press, 1963.)

so, basic relaxation exercises can be pursued quite well in straight chairs or even in wheelchairs. The leader should never allow handicaps to prevent a group member from participating in each basic activity, however it must be modified because of lost mobility or sensory powers.

Concentration is the keystone of improvisational work. In various workshops, however, I have observed that some seniors, especially older seniors in residential settings, seem to practice what might be called *generalized concentration.* That is, they are satisfied to grasp a stimulus approximately instead of exactly. This can be seen, for example, in mirror exercises during which the mirroring partner is content to wave an arm generally although the modeling partner is making a very specific gesture. Perhaps this generalized concentration reflects the feeling that one is no longer responsible for doing things to a very high standard; or perhaps passive activities like TV watching put such a low premium on exact comprehension that powers of concentration atrophy. In either case, regular and continual concentration exercises should be used to push toward high standards of perception and response.

Exterior concentration, of course, depends on the senses. But physiological changes, environmental sensory deprivation, or changed life habits may diminish the sensory powers of senior adults. Workshop activities can do nothing about the first cause, but a basic value of improvisational drama is its ability to address the latter two influences. Thus, each session should include sensory awareness exercises, especially those which require the participants to express precisely what their senses

Jolantha Kershschnagel and Tony Moscoto of the Brookdale Drama Project, in New York City, use props to inspire improvisation by senior adults. (Photo by Glen Faber, courtesy of Milton Polsky)

discover. Way offers an effective listening exercise in which participants listen first for sounds outside the meeting room, then inside, then next to themselves, and finally within themselves, thereafter describing what they have heard to the rest of the group.[8] Even seniors with diminished sensory capacities can increase their confidence in their remaining abilities through such exercises.

A final important area for attention is memory work, an activity specially relevant to seniors. Not only do they have more memories than younger persons, but the past is one of their best sources of

8. Way, 17–18.

50

material and inspiration. Chicago's Free Street Too company bases its very effective production on its members' painful and pleasurable memories of the twentieth century. Some school districts have developed programs in which senior adults present their recollections to students as oral history. By thus employing their memories of things past, we place a value on the lives of our senior citizens, some of whom may have begun to value themselves less. A drama program could hardly accomplish anything better.

Performance

Whether improvisational drama activities should lead to public performance is a matter of some debate in the field. If you lead senior adults, however, your group will probably take the matter out of your hands. If they decide they wish to perform, and they probably will, there should be no shortage of opportunities, beginning with lunchtime shows at congregate meal centers and including visits to nursing homes, retirement centers, schools and clubs.

It may be that your group will push to perform before you want them to. If so, don't be disturbed; friendly audiences will greet them warmly, and that response will achieve in large measure one of

your primary goals—raising group morale. Kubie
and Landau reported that dramatic performances
were milestones in the history of their senior day
center, because they were the first activities to
earn real attention from the outside community.
By earning that attention, the senior players won
status and admiration within their center.[9]

Leadership over the Long Haul

A final question: how long should your leadership
be necessary? Shouldn't adults, after all, develop
toward independence in any activity? Indeed, this
author has seen senior adults absorb, in six weeks
of thrice-weekly sessions, sufficient basic skills to
continue without outside leadership. However,
more important than what a group can do may be
what it *thinks* it can do. If a group lacks confidence
in its independent abilities, the withdrawal of
leadership may lead to absenteeism and decline.
And, largely because of messages received from
society at large, many seniors tend to doubt their
independent powers, especially in activities tried
first after retirement. It's probably a good idea,
therefore, to reduce but not eliminate your
leadership contribution. The group that has met

9. Susan Kubie and Gertrude Landau, *Group Work with the
Aged* (New York: International Universities Press, Inc., 1969.)

for a few sessions on its own will feel revitalized and motivated by a visit from a trusted friend and leader. And for older seniors living in a retirement or nursing home, the occasional visit of the workshop leader will be a happy social event.

If you do have to leave your group, an ideal way to assure the continuity of dramatic activity might be to convince a center staff member with a warm, lively personality to enroll in creative drama courses at a nearby university so that he or she could take over as drama leader. Indeed, there will probably always be a shortage of theatre professionals with the time, personality, and inclination to bring drama work into senior clubs and centers. It's to be hoped, therefore, that in order to qualify senior service professionals as drama leaders, many universities will soon offer special continuing education courses in senior adult improvisational drama. Obviously, seniors themselves may take advantage of such courses and become leaders of their own groups.

V

Serving Senior Adult Audiences

C. Robert Kase

The theatre experience should be available to all senior adults. Some will find creative participation neither desirable nor possible, but with few exceptions, they can attend theatre performances by school, college, community, professional, or senior adult theatre groups in their area.

However, many seniors have reached retirement age without having developed a taste for the live theatre experience. They will not suddenly change lifetime patterns of behavior unless producers actively court their attendance and make theatregoing seem both attractive and easy.

The most obvious way to get senior adults to the theatre is by offering special inducements such as free or reduced-price tickets. To producers whose theatres have financial problems of one kind or another, this suggestion may seem at first unfeasible. But consider it from the standpoint of filling unsold seats. Very few theatres play to capacity; among all but the most successful, eighty per cent of a house is considered good. Why not fill the empty twenty per cent of your seats by making them available at reduced rates to seniors and give your casts the pleasure of playing to full houses? If you are already playing to capacity, add performances and thus build an even larger audience than you had before. Don't allow an unsold seat to become an empty seat.

Distributing free or reduced-price tickets to seniors can be handled in several ways. You can arbitrarily set aside a certain number of free or reduced-price tickets in advance. Some theatres that do so reserve the right to withdraw those tickets at any time when the demand for regular paid admissions becomes too great. This option protects box office income, but it should be exercised only when absolutely necessary.

To build your senior adult audience successfully, you need to promote the sale or distribution of tickets just as you would to increase your draw of any other segment of the potential audience. You'll need to make direct contacts with retirement homes and centers, senior adult organizations like local chapters of the American Association of Retired Persons, the National Retired Teachers Association, or Golden Age Clubs. You can obtain address lists from your local Office on Aging. With luck, you will be able to arrange theatre parties through the social directors of these groups.

But don't neglect your regular sources of publicity—the local newspapers and broadcast stations—for these will reach not only senior groups, but many of the senior adults that are not associated with these groups, who may need the theatre experience even more than affiliated ones.

Many universities operate free or low-cost ticket programs for seniors. Prominent among them is the University of Delaware, whose 2,000-member Over 65 Club has been in existence since 1972. The Club members, alumni over sixty-five, receive membership cards which entitle them to free admission to theatre and music performances, films, lectures, and other cultural events. Central administration of the system by the University's Division of Continuing Education frees individual departments such as the University Theatre from the administrative burden and allows centralized communication to senior adults.

In Omaha, the Magic Theatre admits senior adults to any performance for fifty cents, and in Jackson, Mississippi, the New State Theatre not only provides free senior tickets but transports senior groups and offers after-show senior adult seminars.

The importance of reduced-price ticket programs cannot be overestimated. In inflationary times, only the most affluent retired persons have liberal entertainment budgets. When Proposition Thirteen forced California university box offices to charge seniors for tickets that had previously been given free, an immediate fall-off in senior attendance was noted.

But reducing ticket prices will not of itself bring your theatre to all the senior adults who might enjoy it. For many seniors, transportation is a limiting factor, especially at night. Perhaps, like Jackson's theatre, you can provide transportation. But if

The Senior Acting Troupe of the Barn Players Theatre fills one of its 100-plus bookings from its base at Johnson County Community College, Shawnee Mission, Kansas.

your budget precludes that, there's a good chance that cooperation with local agencies will produce transportation assistance. Meals on Wheels operations, for example, have transportation networks, as do many senior citizen centers and retirement homes. The aggressive soliciting of theatre parties from such organizations may resolve senior transportation problems.

Finally, you should recognize that many senior adults prefer to go out only in the daytime. Indeed, because of fear of crime, the greater difficulty of obtaining transportation, and other factors, so many seniors will not come out at night that you may do well to consider adding a special matinee to be promoted as a senior citizen or special audience event. Or you might invite senior adults to classroom and experimental productions and thus provide a mature reaction to supplement the reactions of the younger students who are usually the staple audience for these performances.

But in the final analysis, some of your potential senior adult audience will not come to you. Older nursing home residents and less adventuresome senior center members form an important audience that you can only reach by touring.

Indeed, touring has become a salient feature of senior adult theatre; a great many senior companies and a few younger groups now design productions expressly for touring to congregate centers for the elderly. Several professional theatres, including the Guthrie of Minneapolis and the Actors Theatre of Louisville, have organized senior companies specifically for touring. And the best known college-sponsored senior group, Maryland's Au-

An all-male cast of The Canterbury Players, based in Tampa, Florida, takes a curtain call after performing *Pyramus and Thisbe* under Bob Kase's direction.

tumn Players, made its impact primarily by touring to nutrition centers. In Tampa, the Canterbury Players, a retirement center company, regularly takes its productions to other retirement communities. Any company prepared to offer short, simple productions to senior centers will find no shortage of takers. Portland, Oregon's Theatre of Feast, a company ranging in age from 72 to 96, has not only toured widely in Oregon, but has played in California, Texas, Idaho, and Washington.

Senior touring should be kept extremely simple. A lunchtime bill can be developed around a set of small-cast one-act plays, which may be offered together or singly depending on the length of presentation that best suits the host organization.

Lightness and simplicity of production should characterize senior adult touring. From Northridge, California, the Theatre for Senior Performers reports that it tours one-act plays using "three screens, a table, and two chairs for scenery." And in the Philadelphia suburbs, the Third Age Theatre carries a few portable screens and boxes of props in the back of a station wagon. To set their stage, the Third Agers use furniture found at the tour site. In all senior adult theatre, the emphasis is on the performer, so such minimally mounted performances are greeted with great enthusiasm by their host audiences.

Whether the show goes to the senior audience or vice versa, production planners are well advised to include provisions for after-show discussion, especially if the play has some bearing on the experience of growing older. Some senior theatre groups, such as San Francisco's Tale Spinners and New York's Theatre for Older People, an offshoot of the Joseph Jefferson Theatre Company, produce original plays relevant to the aging experience in order to encourage their audiences to explore the issues involved, after the performance.

Some theatre purists may question making a play a launching pad for discussion on the ground that it makes the play itself less than "the thing." On the other hand, post-show debate makes the audience an active participant in the theatre experience, and replacing passivity with activity should be a basic goal of all senior adult art programs.[1]

1. In all fairness it should be observed that most senior citizens do not attend theatre for the purpose of discussing their problems. On the other hand, they may enjoy a humorous treatment of their difficulties such as is found in the presentation of the absurdities of memory lapses in *I'm Herbert*.

Whether amateur or professional, whatever the ages of its members, every theatre group can and should make specific provision for serving senior adults. Such service may not involve financial sacrifice, indeed, may even be profitable. In any case, the theatre that ignores senior audiences today is seriously out of step with the times and should quickly accommodate itself to the fastest growing segment of its potential audience.

VI

Plays for Senior Adult Production

Loren Winship

The plays recommended below represent the experience of directors and members of senior adult theatre workshops and groups from all over the country. It should not be supposed that all the plays listed are about the elderly; are based on themes pertinent to aging; or call for entirely or mainly senior casts. Their common characteristic is that all the plays have been found useful by senior groups, either for actual productions or for readings.

Some attempt, however, has been made to exclude plays which would present inordinate difficulties to senior adult groups. Lavish musicals, plays concentrating on the affairs of teenagers and young adults, and plays with complicated production requirements have been avoided.

In general, the author has chosen not to include many non-royalty plays because, except for plays which have passed into the public domain with age, the quality of non-royalty plays tends to be doubtful.

One of the things any senior adult theatre group should do upon its formation is to obtain a shelf of play catalogs. Such catalogs, generally available free, will be particularly valuable in that they will include plot summaries of the plays in the following list. At the minimum, catalogs should be obtained from the publishers listed at the end of the play directory.

Whether it is done in full-fledged production or script-in-hand reading, the performance of a play before an audience usually requires the purchase of scripts (it is illegal to duplicate copyright material) and the payment of a royalty. Long plays may be purchased for about $2 to $3 per copy and short plays for between $1 and $2. Royalty fees for short play performances run from $5 to $25 per performance, and those for long plays run from about $25 to $50 per performance. The publishers' catalogs will give complete details on all script and royalty costs.

Under certain conditions, the payment of performance royalties may be waived for senior adult groups. For example, if the play is to be performed only before members of the senior adult theatre group itself or before an audience comprised solely of senior adults, such as the membership of an AARP chapter or a retirement home, some publishers may waive or reduce the fee. But requests for such a royalty waiver should always be made in advance and the justification for such a waiver be clearly stated. Actually, even if you plan to pay the royalty, you should seek performance permission well in advance of the performance date. It is illegal to produce a play without advance permission.

When writing publishers about royalty payments, reductions, or remissions, include the number of performances planned and their dates, the types of audiences, the seating capacity of the theatre or theatres, the proposed ticket prices if tickets are to be sold, and approximate box office receipts, if any, from past performances. Remember, not even senior groups are freed of royalty responsibilities merely by electing not to charge admission to a show. The fact that a group is not charging for tickets may indeed influence a publisher to waive a royalty fee, but that decision is the publisher's and no one else's.

In the following list of plays, the term *comedy* covers farce, all types of comedy, and light mysteries. The term *drama* covers all plays which are principally serious or tragic. After the author's name in each entry, there follows a letter or letters in parentheses; those letters refer to the six publishers listed following the play list. The few plays which do not require the payment of a royalty fee under any circumstances are designated as *non-royalty* immediately following the publisher's code.

Long Plays

Title, Author	Publisher	Type	Cast
All the Way Home, Mosel	F	Comedy	6M7W
Angel Street, Hamilton	B	Drama	2M3W
An Inspector Calls, Priestley	DPS	Drama	4M3W
Anybody Out There?, Patrick	DPS	Comedy	7M3W
Arsenic and Old Lace, Kesselring	DPS	Comedy	11M3W
Blithe Spirit, Coward	F	Comedy	2M5W
Breath of Spring, Coke	F	Comedy	3M5W
Browning Version, The, Rattigan	F	Drama	5M3W
Chalk Garden, The, Bagnold	F	Drama	2M7W
Charley's Aunt, Thomas	F	Comedy	6M4W

Title	Source	Type	Cast
Come Back, Little Sheba, Inge	F	Drama	8M3W
Corn Is Green, The, Williams	DPS	Comedy	10M5W
Craig's Wife, Kelly	F	Drama	5M6W
Curious Savage, The, Patrick	DPS	Comedy	5M5W
Dangerous Corner, Priestley	F	Drama	3M4W
David and Lisa, Reach	F	Drama	11M11W
Desk Set, The, Marchant	F	Comedy	8M8W
Diary of Anne Frank, The, Goodrich & Hackett	DPS	Drama	5M5W
Don't Drink the Water, Allen	F	Comedy	12M4W
Enter Laughing, Stein	F	Comedy	7M4W
Everybody Loves Opal, Patrick	DPS	Comedy	4M2W
Firebugs, The, Frisch	F	Comedy	6M3W
Forty Carats, Allen	F	Comedy	5M6W

Title	Publisher	Genre	Cast
Fourposter, The, de Hartog	F	Comedy	1M1W
Fresh Fields, Novello	F	Comedy	3M6W
Front Page, The, Hecht & Macarthur	F	Comedy	17M5W
Girls in 509, The, Teichmann	F	Comedy	9M3W
Glass Menagerie, The, Williams	DPS	Drama	2M2W
Good Morning, Miss Dove, McCleery	F	Drama	12M10W
Grandma Steps Out, Keeler	DPS	Comedy	5M9W
Great Big Doorstep, The, Goodrich & Hackett	DPS	Comedy	5M7W
Great Sebastians, The, Lindsay & Crouse	DPS	Comedy	15M6W
Harvey, Chase	DPS	Comedy	6M6W
Haunting of Hill House, The, Leslie	DPS	Drama	3M4W
Heaven Can Wait, Segall	DPS	Comedy	7M4W
Heiress, The, Goetz	DPS	Drama	3M6W

Title	Publisher	Type	Cast
Heritage, Barry	F	Drama	7M5W
Importance of Being Earnest, The, Wilde	F, non-royalty	Comedy	5M4W
I Never Sang For My Father, Anderson	DPS	Drama	7M4W
In the Summer House, Bowles	DPS	Drama	5M10W
I Remember Mama, van Druten	DPS	Comedy	9M13W
Jane, Behrman	F	Comedy	5M4W
Ladies In Retirement, Percy & Denham	DPS	Drama	1M6W
Ladies of the Jury, Ballard	F	Comedy	12M10W
Last of the Red Hot Lovers, Simon	F	Comedy	1M3W
Lavender and Old Lace, Warner	F	Comedy	4M6W
Life With Father, Lindsay & Crouse	DPS	Comedy	8M8W
Life With Mother, Lindsay & Crouse	DPS	Comedy	8M8W
Lilies of the Field, The, Leslie	DPS	Drama	4M5W

Little Foxes, The, Hellman	DPS	Drama	6M4W
Living Room, The, Greene	F	Drama	2M5W
Magnificent Obsession, The, Vreeland	B	Drama	5M5W
Middle of the Night, Chayefsky	F	Drama	3M8W
Midgie Purvis, Chase	DPS	Comedy	8M8W
Miser, The, Moliere (Miles Malleson)	F	Comedy	11M3W
Miss Pell is Missing, Gershe	F	Drama	4M3W
Morning's At Seven, Osborn	F	Comedy	4M5W
Mousetrap, The, Christie	F	Comedy	5M3W
Mrs. McThing, Chase	DPS	Comedy	9M10W
My Three Angels, Spewack	DPS	Comedy	7M3W
Never Too Late, Long	F	Comedy	6M3W
Night Must Fall, Williams	F	Drama	4M5W
Night of Jan. 16, Rand	B	Comedy	11M10W

Title	Publisher	Type	Cast
Old Maid, The, Akins	F	Drama	5M9W
Our Town, Wilder	F	Drama	17M7W
Patterns, Reach	F	Drama	7M6W
Photo Finish, Ustinov	DPS	Comedy	6M5W
Plaza Suite, Simon	F	Comedy	3M2W
Potting Shed, The, Greene	F	Comedy	6M5W
Promenade All, Robison	F	Comedy	3M1W
Sabrina Fair, Taylor	DPS	Comedy	7M7W
Send Me No Flowers, Barasch & Moore	F	Comedy	9M3W
Separate Tables, Rattigan	F	Drama	3M8W
Seven Nuns At Las Vegas, White	DPS	Comedy	2M11W
Silver Whistle, The, McEnroe	DPS	Comedy	10M5W
Sleuth, Shaffer	F	Comedy	2M
Solid Gold Cadillac, The, Teichmann & Kaufman	DPS	Comedy	11M6W

Title	Publisher	Genre	Cast
Southwest Corner, The, Holm	DPS	Comedy	3M4W
Spofford, Shumlin	F	Comedy	9M9W
Spoon River Anthology, Aidman	F	Drama	3M2W
Steambath, Friedman	F	Drama	12M2W
Strange Bedfellows, Ryerson & Clements	F	Comedy	7M11W
Subject Was Roses, The, Gilroy	F	Drama	2M1W
Suspect, Percy & Denham	DPS	Drama	4M4W
Ten Little Indians, Christie	F	Drama	8M3W
Tenth Man, The, Chayefsky	F	Comedy	12M1W
That's Where the Town's Going, Mosel	DPS	Drama	2M2W
Time For Elizabeth, Krasna & Marx	DPS	Comedy	8M6W
Trip to Bountiful, The, Foote	DPS	Drama	6M3W
Twelve Angry Men (or Women), Rose	DPS	Drama	12M(12W)

Title	Publisher	Genre	Cast
Under Milkwood, Thomas	F	Drama	17M17W
Visit to a Small Planet, Vidal	DPS	Comedy	8M2W
Waiting for Godot, Beckett	DPS	Drama	5M
Waltz of the Toreadors, The, Anouilh	F	Comedy	4M7W
Who'll Save the Plowboy?, Gilroy	F	Drama	4M2W
Witness for the Prosecution, Christie	F	Drama	17M5W
Wooden Dish, The, Morris	DPS	Drama	6M4W
You Can't Take It With You, Hart & Kaufman	DPS	Comedy	9M7W

Short Plays

Title, Author	Publisher	Type	Cast
Adaptation, May	DPS	Comedy	3M1W
Ah, Romance, Hackett	B	Comedy	8W
Ah, Sweet Mystery, Kirkpatrick	F	Comedy	3M5W
American Dream, The, Albee	DPS	Comedy	2M3W
Apollo of Bellac, Giraudoux	F	Comedy	9M3W
At a Beetle's Pace, Catron	B	Comedy	1M1W
Bald Soprano, The, Ionesco	F	Comedy	3M3W
Bathroom Door, The, Jennings	F	Comedy	3M3W
Bespoke Overcoat, The, Mankowitz	F	Drama	4M
Bishop's Candlesticks, The, McKinnel	F	Drama	3M2W

Boor, The, Chekhov	F, non-royalty	Comedy	2M1W
Box and Cox, Morton	F, non-royalty	Comedy	2M1W
Candle On the Table, A, Clapp	B	Comedy	4W
Chairs, The, Ionesco	F	Drama	2M1W
Conquest of Everest, The, Kopit	F	Comedy	2M1W
Court Martial of Billy Budd, The, Salem	DPC	Drama	11M
Dark Lady of the Sonnets, The, Shaw	F	Drama	2M2W
Day It Rained Forever, The, Bradburg	F	Comedy	3M1W
Dear Departed, The, Houghton	F	Comedy	3M3W
Death of the Hired Man, The, Gould	DPC	Drama	2M2W
Death of the Old Man, Foote	DPS	Drama	4M3W
Devil and Daniel Webster, The, Benet	DPS	Comedy	6M1W
Dipper, The, Murth	B	Comedy	4W

Dust of the Road, Goodman	F	Drama	3M1W
Dutch Treat, Lynch	F	Comedy	1M1W
End of the Beginning, O'Casey	F	Comedy	2M1W
Farce of the Worthy Master Pierre Patelin, Jagendorf	B	Comedy	4M1W
Finders-Keepers, Kelly	F	Drama	1M2W
Finger of God, The, Wilde	B	Drama	2M1W
Fishing Hat, The, Lynch	F	Comedy	1M1W
Flattering Word, The, Kelly	F	Drama	2M3W
Florence Unlimited, Carmichael	B	Comedy	6W
Florist Shop, The, Hawkridge	B	Comedy	3M2W
Fumed Oak, Coward	F	Comedy	1M3W
Game of Chess, The, Goodman	F	Drama	4M
Gloria Mundi, Brown	F	Drama	2M4W

Title	Publisher	Genre	Cast
Granny's Little Cheery Room, Conkle	F	Comedy	1M3W
Hands Across the Sea, Coward	F	Comedy	6M3W
Happy Journey to Camden and Trenton, The, Wilder	F	Comedy	3M3W
Hello Out There, Saroyan	F	Drama	3M2W
Heritage of Wimpole Street, The, Knippe	B	Drama	2M3W
Hitch-Hiker, The, Fletcher	DPS	Drama	4M8W
If Men Played Cards As Women Do, Kaufman	F	Comedy	4M
In the Gloaming, Oh My Darling, Terry	F	Drama	4M6W
In the Shadow of the Glen, Synge	F	Drama	3M1W
Joint Owners in Spain, Brown	B	Comedy	4W
Kissing Sweet, Guare	DPS	Comedy	2M2W
Ladies of the Mop, Harris	B, non-royalty	Comedy	4W
Last of Sherlock Holmes, The, Kelley	B	Comedy	2M3W

Let Me Hear You Whisper, Zindel	DPS	Comedy	5W
Lord Byron's Love Letter, Williams	DPS	Drama	1M3W
Lottery, The, Duffield	DPC	Drama	8M5W
Maker of Dreams, The, Down	F	Comedy	2M1W
Man in the Bowler Hat, The, Milne	F	Comedy	4M1W
Marriage Proposal, The, Chekhov	F, non-royalty	Comedy	2M1W
Minnie Field, Conkle	F	Drama	5M
Minuet, A, Parker	F	Drama	5M
Miser, The, Moliere (1 act)	A	Comedy	10M4W
Monkey's Paw, The, Jacobs & Parker	F	Drama	4M1W
Mooncalf Mugford, Duffield & Leary	DPC	Drama	2M3W
Mr. Flannery's Ocean, Carlino	DPS	Comedy	3M5W
Mrs. Ritter Appears, Kelly	F	Comedy	1M4W

Neighbors, The, Gale	B	Comedy	2M6W
Nellie Was a Lady, Kirkpatrick	F	Comedy	2M5W
Old Lady Shows Her Medals, The, Barrie	F	Comedy	2M4W
Opening Night, Fernand	DPC	Comedy	1M10W
Outcasts of Poker Flat, The, Edwards	DPC	Drama	4M3W
Over the Teacups, Wilde	B	Comedy	4W
Overtones, Gerstenberg	M	Comedy	4W
Patchwork Quilt, The, Field	F	Comedy	2M5W
Pearls, Tothero	F	Comedy	2M2W
People in the Glass Paperweight, The, McKinney	B	Comedy	2M1W
Poor Aubrey, Kelly	B	Comedy	1M3W
Potboiler, The, Gerstenberg	M	Comedy	5M2W
Pullman Car Hiawatha, Wilder	F	Comedy	15M18W

Purple Doorknob, The, Eaton	F	Comedy	3W
Queens of France, Wilder	F	Comedy	1M3W
Quiet Please, Bauermann	DPS	Comedy	3M4W
Rehearsal, Morley	M	Comedy	6W
Riders to the Sea, Synge	B	Drama	3M3W
Shall We Join the Ladies, Barrie	F	Drama	8M8W
She Married Well, Kirkpatrick	F	Comedy	3M3W
Short Walk After Dinner, A, Haubold	F	Drama	1M2W
Shut Up, Martha, Haubold	B	Comedy	3M1W
Sisters McIntosh, The, Carson	F	Comedy	1M2W
Something Unspoken, Williams	DPS	Drama	2W
So Nice Not to See You, Carmichael	F	Comedy	7W
Sparkin', Conkle	F	Comedy	1M3W

Summer People, The, Jackson	DPC	Drama	4M3W
Suppressed Desires, Glaspell	B	Drama	1M2W
Thirty Minutes in a Street, Mayor	F	Comedy	12M11W
This Way to Heaven, Parkhurst	F	Comedy	2M2W
Three On a Bench, Estrada	F	Comedy	2M2W
Traveling Sisters, The, Kirkpatrick	F	Comedy	3M4W
Trifles, Glaspell	B	Drama	3M2W
Undercurrent, The, Ehlert	F	Drama	2M4W
Whisper Into My Good Ear, Hanley	DPS	Drama	2M
Why I Am a Bachelor, Seiler	DPS	Comedy	2M4W
Will, The, Barrie	F	Comedy	6M1W
Workhouse Ward, The, Gregory	F	Comedy	2M1W

Plays For Special Occasions

Title, Author	Publisher	Type	Cast
Animal Farm, Orwell, Reading, full-length	F	Comedy	5M2W
Between Two Thieves, LeRoy, Biblical, full-length	F	Drama	9M4W
Christ in the Concrete City, Turner, Biblical, one-act	F	Drama	4M2W
Cradle Song, The, Martinez-Sierra, Religious, full-length	F	Comedy	4M10W
Family Portrait, Coffee & Cowen, Biblical, full-length	F	Drama	12M10W
Fortune Teller, The, Wilson & Bradley, Musical, full-length	B, non-royalty	Comedy	10M6W

Title	Publisher	Type	Cast
Gift of the Magi, The, Martens, Christmas, one-act	DPC	Comedy	2M5W
Journey of the Star, The, Murch, Christmas, one-act	B	Comedy	7W
No Name In the Street, Murch, Easter, one-act	B	Drama	8M14W
Saint Germaine, Murch, Christmas, one-act	B	Drama	5W
Telemachus Clay, Carolino, Morality, full-length	DPS	Drama	7M4W
Tell It to the Wind, Murch, Christmas, one-act	B	Comedy	7W
Terrible Meek, The, Ronn, Biblical, one-act	F, non-royalty	Drama	2M1W

Play Collections

An Evening of One-Act Stagers for Golden Agers, Albert M. Brown, F. These plays are short and easy to stage. They do not require a great deal of action and can also be used as readings.

Short Plays for the Long Living, Roger Cornish, B. Six short plays, each with two characters. In each play a long-living man or woman runs head-on into the roadblocks life seems to provide for the senior citizen—and comes out of the collision intact, if bruised and wiser.

Publishers List

(A) Anchorage Press, 4621 Charles Avenue, New Orleans, La. 70115

(B) Baker's Plays, 100 Chauncey St., Boston, Mass. 02111

(M) David McKay, 750 Third Ave., New York, N. Y. 10017

(DPC) Dramatic Publishing Company, 86 E. Randolph St., Chicago, Il. 60601

(DPS) Dramatists Play Service, Inc., 440 Park Ave., S., New York, N. Y. 10016

(F) Samuel French, Inc., 25 W. 45th St., New York, N. Y. 10036

(P) Pioneer Drama Service, P. O. Box 22555, Denver, Col. 80222

New Unpublished Plays

The following new, unpublished plays have either been sent to me or have been brought to my attention as Chairman of the ATA Senior Adult Theatre Program Committee. The listing does not necessarily indicate a recommendation of the plays. If interested, one should write to the playwright at the address given. Editor's Note (CRK)

Long Plays

On the Boardwalk of Atlantic City, Emily McGlinchey, Musical Comedy, two acts, 4M5W (variable). A singing chorus of variable size sings many old familiar songs. Between the songs are short skits (3 to 5 minutes). This entertaining and amusing musical was produced by the Newark (Delaware) Senior Center Players, as were two similar shows by the same playwright, *America, Of*

Thee I Sing and *Those Wonderful Years.* (Write Emily McGlinchey, 76 Welsh Tract Rd., Apt. 304, Newark, Del. 19713.

Evening Star, Howard Richardson and Francis Goforth, Comedy-Drama, three acts, 5M5W. Old passions flare in a retirement home for actors and actresses. This play had its world premiere in Kingsport, Tennessee, in 1977, and scenes from it were presented on NBC-TV in 1979 by the New Dimension Theatre of New Haven. (Write Howard Richardson, 207 Columbus Ave., New York, N. Y. 10023.)

This Way to the Egress, Bill Burnett, Comedy, two acts, 4M4W. A group of senior citizens gathers at a community center to produce a play. The playwright has a keen sense of humor and keeps the situation in amusing turmoil throughout. (Write Bill Burnett, 37 Lewis St., Suite 806, Hartford, Conn. 06103.)

Short Plays

The Boarding House, College Avenue Players, 1M4W. A group of women adjusts to life in a retirement center. (Write College Avenue Players, Stuart Kendall, Director, 546 Crofton Ave., Oakland, Calif. 94610.)

Emma's Dilemma, Mimi Haessler, 3W. A wealthy widow, dissatisfied with her home and maid, arranges to move into a retirement center, only to discover that her maid is moving to the same place.

The Wednesday Bridge Club, or *How Men Think Women Play Bridge,* Mimi Haessler, 4M. A male foursome behave and talk as they believe their wives do at the bridge table. (Write Mimi Haessler, 16-A Millwood Rd., Mid Florida Lakes, Leesburg, Fla. 32748.)

Magic Time, Elyse Nass. A comedy-drama produced at the Quaigh Theatre and various senior centers in New York. (Write Elyse Nass, 60-10 47th Ave., Woodside, N.Y. 11377.)

Short Plays by Irene Paul. An intriguing group of titles: *Let Her Eat Cake, The Blessings of Solomon, Alone, Night Editor, The X-Rated Grandmother, The Absolute Man, Mr. Sawbucks and the Pollster,* and *Can Dead Men Cry?* (Write Irene Paul, 2063 28th Ave., San Francisco, Calif. 94116.)

VII

Budgets for Senior Adult Theatre

C. Robert Kase

In at least one way, senior adult theatre groups are no different from any other kind—money is a consideration. It is true, of course, that senior adult theatre operations are likely to be less expensive than others in several ways: its performers won't expect to be paid except under exceptional circumstances; nor is senior adult theatre given to extravagant physical productions.

The earlier chapters should give one a general idea of the nature of the expenses involved in each type of SAT project, and your trained and experienced director can fill in the details.

Of one thing you can be certain, there will be expenses, however small.

Expenses

Fortunately, most groups can keep their expenses truly low. The improvisational group will manage on very little outlay at all; it requires neither special settings nor purchased scripts. The few props that an improvisational group may need will be gathered from its members' kitchens and attics; its costumes will be on its backs.

Even the staged production will cost very little if the script is intelligently chosen and the director remembers that performance, not scenic display, is the essence of senior adult theatre.

The basic costs that must be considered in advance for senior adult theatre are three: scripts and royalties; direction if a qualified volunteer director is not available; and production.

The matter of paying for scripts and royalties—as well as applying for reductions or remissions—is addressed at length in Chapter VI. It need merely be observed here that the popularity of one-act plays among senior groups will tend to keep royalties low. Those groups which produce original plays from their own playwriting workshops also avoid royalty and purchase costs, although they do have the smaller costs involved with typing and copying scripts. Even if relatively high-royalty plays are used, however, that cost can usually be recovered with a modest ticket charge. Unless a group elects to do musicals, and few senior groups do full-scale musical comedies, the highest royalty fee for a long play is likely to be $50 for the first performance and less for succeeding performances. One-act play royalties usually run from $5 to $15 per performance.

The cost of direction is more problematic. According to the ATA Senior Adult Theatre Project Report, the single purpose for which money is

88

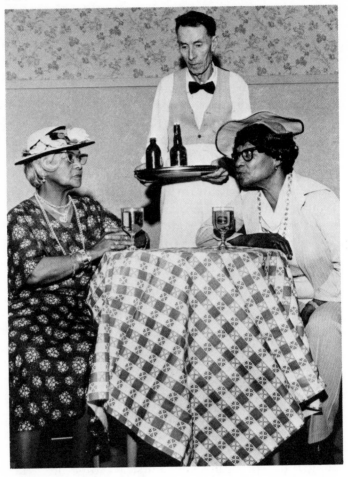

A simple set works well in a scene from *Friends and Lovers*, produced by the College Avenue Players of Oakland, California. (Photo by Bob Doty)

most often needed is the payment of a director. As has been made clear elsewhere in this *Handbook,* a qualified director must be used if a senior program is to have a good chance of success. If a capable director does not emerge from within the group, an outsider will have to be found, either on a volunteer or a paid basis.

Obviously, seeking a qualified volunteer is a wise course to start with. The group should contact the local school, college, or community theatre for possible candidates. Often community theatre members with wide experience would like the opportunity to direct, which may not have been afforded them by their local theatres. Because they make their living by other means, such persons may well be willing to direct for the joy of it; they will not feel they are giving away their professional bread and butter. Similarly, advanced college students might also volunteer for the sake of getting some experience. For many such directors, the only reward necessary is a good performance, the feeling that he or she has grown creatively, and a modest token of gratitude afterwards.

On the other hand, a group that seeks a long-term commitment from an outside director may have to find a way of compensating that person. Pay need not be high, especially since the time involved may be only a few hours per week. In any case, it is to be hoped that a local college, arts council, or agency for the aged will be able to subsidize such leadership.

In Tampa, Florida, for example, the Community Instructional Services Program of the Continuing Education Division of the Hillsborough

A coming attraction is advertised in a senior activities center by the Third Age Theatre of Ambler, Pennsylvania.

County Public Schools supports a series of theatre workshops in Retirement Centers. The laboratory part of the workshops involves the rehearsal and performance of a play or the development of an improvisational program.

Another potential source of directing leadership may be in the Corps of ATA Retirees being organized by the Senior Adult Theatre Program Committee. As this Corps grows, it can provide more and more of the skilled directors needed by the SAT Program.

Most senior groups manage without paying significant production costs. They are content to produce plays in ordinary rooms with a few pieces of furniture comprising the scenery. If they are fortunate enough to have a small stage for traditional plays, so much the better. Under certain circumstances, however, the available space makes it impossible to perform without some kind of stage; without it, actors simply cannot be seen or heard. In such a case, a group would do well to either build or rent simple platforms to provide the necessary elevation, as noted in Chapter III. Portable platforms may be collapsed for storage when not in use.

Whether producing on a stage or on the floor, most groups will do well to limit scenery to simple screens and borrowed furniture. Not only will this policy save money, it will allow more frequent, varied, and tourable productions.

Except for the most advanced groups and those sponsored by established theatres or university theatre departments, most senior groups forgo the use of special lighting. The cost here would be prohibitive for most groups, and the value of advanced stage lighting is lessened anyway because many senior groups perform in the daytime in spaces which are seldom truly dark.

Sources of Income

If a group is not so fortunate as to receive some operating income automatically—from a retirement home activity fund, for example—there are certain basic ways by which it can attempt to get the money it needs for minimum operations. A retirement community theatre whose members are self-sufficient can charge modest dues. At the Mossmore Leisure World Community of Silver Springs, Maryland, 140 members of the theatre group, Fun and Fancy, pay $3.00 annual dues and thus provide a comfortable base for their work. For groups that produce with minimal trappings, dues may be even more modest.

When public performances are offered, an obvious way to make money is by charging an admission fee or requesting a voluntary contribution from audience members as museums often do. Service organizations or businesses may accept invitations to act as sponsors—the latter for advertising or public relations purposes.

Some senior groups that tour to nursing homes, churches, and other centers charge the host organization a small booking fee. Portland, Oregon's Theatre of Feast, a leader among touring groups, derives its entire income from tour fees. Lest one think that senior groups are limited to tiny bits of income, it should be pointed out that Chicago's Free Street Too asks and gets $500 per tour performance and adds that income to other financing, which includes Comprehensive Employment Training Act funding from the federal government. Free Street Too, of course, pays its senior performers—there is no absolute limit to the range of senior adult theatre.

From my files on Senior Adult Theatre Projects I have found the following varied sources of financial support: CETA, senior centers, trust funds, State Departments of Health, senior departments of YMHAs, State Offices of Aging, various Federal programs for the elderly, a life insurance company, a Bicentennial Commission, a church, and a Community Recreation Department. The above were selected at random.

For financial support of small projects, local sources will probably be adequate. Many organizations are anxious and willing to help senior citizen activities: service clubs, churches, fraternal organizations, all kinds of community organizations, state and community recreation departments, to mention only a few. You might consult government and private senior citizen organizations for leads. Sources of support will vary with the community. There is a strong desire to assist any project which can make the lives of our elder citizens more complete and satisfying.

A word of advice: before seeking support from an individual or agency, try to get some exposure for your SAT project in the press, radio, and/or television. In making your pitch for backing, you have an advantage if people have already heard about your project.

Before approaching an agency for money, it is wise to consult the agency to see if there is any special form to be used and to identify any limitations on the kind of funding provided. And by all means enlist the aid of an experienced grant proposal writer if you can.

Finally, most senior adult groups with substantial programs of public performance eventually try to raise operating funds through grants from outside agencies, public or private. Every state and many cities and counties have agencies concerned with the problems and welfare of the aging. These agencies come with many different labels. In Tampa, Florida, for example, there are the Senior Citizens Nutrition and Activity Program, the County Office on Aging, and the Retired Senior Volunteer Program. You will often find both city and county recreation departments interested in supporting a program of senior adult theatre. A good first step is to consult the Yellow Pages under the headings of federal, state, county, and city agencies. Another important source of assistance is the state arts council; a number of SAT projects are now funded by these. Information useful in the search for funds—sometimes even funds—may be obtained from the organizations and agencies listed following this chapter. Of some help in seeking larger grants may be a pamphlet, *Funding Sources,* containing an extensive list of possible sources as well as suggestions for preparing grant applications (write ARTS, Box 2040, Grand Central Station, New York, N.Y. 10017).

In summary, the financial pictures of senior adult theatre organizations vary widely from the simplest group which can mount a play reading for the pleasure of its members and friends, for a few dollars, to complex organizations like Free Street Too or Boston's New Wrinkle Theatre, which operates on booking fees and a combination of federal and state grants. The size of your budget depends on the size of your ambition.

But, in general, it's safe to say that in no echelon

of the theatre is money less important than in senior adult theatre. For older persons exploring a new world of art and pleasure, enthusiasm and fellowship are the only real coin of the realm.

Agencies and Organizations

American Theatre Association Senior Adult Theatre Program Committee, 1000 Vermont Avenue, N. W., Washington, D. C. 20005.

Administration on Aging, Office of Human Development, Department of Health, Education, and Welfare, Washington, D. C. 20201. (funding)

Expansion Arts Program, National Endowment for the Arts, Washington, D. C. 20506. (funding)

Life Long Learning Project, Department of Health, Education, and Welfare, 608 13th St., N. W., Washington, D. C. 20005.

National Center for the Arts and Aging, National Council on Aging, 1828 L St., N. W., Washington, D. C. 20036.

National Committee on Art Education for the Elderly, Albert Beck, Executive Director, 520-5 Culver-Stockton College, Canton, Mo. 63435.

New England Gerontology Center, 15 Garrison Avenue, Durham, N. H. 03824. (For periodic mailings listing publications on aging.)

Older Workers Program, Office of National Programs, Manpower Administration, Department of

Labor, Patrick Henry Building, 601 D St., N. W., Washington, D. C. 20213. (Subsidizes part-time community service by unemployed.)

Retired Senior Volunteer Program (RSVP), AC-TION, 806 Connecticut Ave., N. W., Washington, D. C. 20525. (funding)